OF CARTOGRAPHY

VOLUME 81

Sun Tracks

An American Indian Literary Series

OF CARTOGRAPHY

poems

ESTHER G. BELIN

THE UNIVERSITY OF
ARIZONA PRESS

TUCSON

The University of Arizona Press
www.uapress.arizona.edu

Printed in the United States of America
22   21   20   19   18   17   6   5   4   3   2   1

ISBN-13: 978-0-8165-3602-3 (paper)

Cover design by Leigh McDonald
Cover art by Esther G. Belin

Publication of this book is made possible in part by the proceeds of a permanent endowment created with the assistance of a Challenge Grant from the National Endowment for the Humanities, a federal agency.

Library of Congress Cataloging-in-Publication Data
Names: Belin, Esther G., author.
Title: Of cartography : poems / Esther G. Belin.
Other titles: Sun tracks ; v. 81.
Description: Tucson : The University of Arizona Press, 2017. | Series: Sun tracks : an American Indian literary series ; volume 81
Identifiers: LCCN 2017003543 | ISBN 9780816536023 (pbk. : alk. paper)
Subjects: | LCGFT: Poetry.
Classification: LCC PS3552.E479627 O35 2017 | DDC 811/.54—dc23 LC record available at https://lccn.loc.gov/2017003543

♾ This paper meets the requirements of ANSI/NISO Z39.48-1992 (Permanence of Paper).

this writing serves as another contribution to the process, the practice of patience & the faithfulness of the Creator of all things

this writing acknowledges two people who remained in sight during the process

1. *Dr. Connie Jacobs — more than a friend: her heartbeat is what you hear as each page is turned*
2. *Frank Hyde — fellow IAIA alum: here is my second book*

this writing is for the Edd girls

CONTENTS

NORTH

OF CARTOGRAPHY

bundles are bundling

názbas

názbas

názbas

názbas

my tongue is a fire
today I am the water
yesterday I was wood

I give my body to the flames
I give my body to the energy that makes me struggle
I give my body to the tomb
where the wind
of the holy spirit
blows in my face

if yesterday I was wood,
I place my tongue onto the kitchen table near the butcher block of knives
if today I am water
I pour my tongue over the hard goods and bodily imprints attached to
mountains

to be restored
I begin this poem with the end in mind
to be restored
I begin this poem with a stone knife in hand
to be restored
I begin this poem with fire

thinning into female mist
the spiral from my skull is tangled in the moon's belly
a zigzag attachment, a breathing entity, coal-fired thoughts
deepening
widening

another moon approaches
like buffalo grass seed germination
thwarted, intact under layers
like Navajo culture, like primitive
chants, like a 12 step ladder

1. Lightness	2. Air – Spaces	3. Dry Land & Separation
Navajos are	People	Arroyos in
Much more than	Fighting us	More than the spirit world
Prayer	Prayer(full) of	Methodology
		I cut a window into walls with
		my prayers
	I use Wi-Fi to connect	
cut the tops off		
the letters of		
my words		
	&	The flood spills across the
		page

Look: silver screens groom the sky, their constant filtering
brings frost, the iridescent paint
Coyote uses
over the low mountain
under the low moon
firmament

Look: this is where mom hid the metal tin containing
all her stick toys, the flat sandstone slivers
bighan still stands

Look: that is what they call Navajo Education

a speaker stand and a microphone
hollow out the air
like cracking a can of pop
the first gulp of
Navajos rotating like
warehoused collections
flattened on a screen
breathing in and in and never out
distortion propelled as Promethean
and people sit quietly, in awe of the striptease
the digital transfers deluge the darkness
a marked deck of images
displayed
and people sit quietly, stirred slightly
from the stripper's blank stare
and they vaguely remember clapping their hands

Building Materials:
1. dawn
2. evening light
3. dark cloud
4. male rain
5. dark mist
6. female rain
7. pollen
8. grasshoppers

hmm, where can I find the grasshoppers?

The Process
After collecting all the building materials, add
the interior ingredients:
1. restore
2. recover
3. "cool" feeling
4. "happily"
5. abundant
6. transformation = from human to: mountains, herbs, fir tree,
   morning mists, clouds, gathering waters, wilderness, dew drops,
   pollen

Next:
Go to your house made of mirage
there you will find the building permit and instructions
there is your story wrapped inside the rainbow

Visibility
not
subjective speculation
excavating the credible
sudden hovering
only the matrix

Invisibility
not
desexualization
structural opposition to savagism
the black printed text on paper

Apricot-Grain Cottage
Roofbeams cut from deep-grained apricot,
fragrant reeds braided into thatched eaves:

no one knows clouds beneath these rafters
drifting off to bring that human realm rain.
                                        —Wang Wei

Yesterday I was wood. Today I am moist with rain, busily figuring out the Cartesian product of my four daughters and my four bad habits. Sometimes I feel like the flood waters. repulsed. accommodating to the antediluvian order. My blank journal begs me to write all over it. everything. twists from anchored cords. mythic tangles. the damp soil from rabbit holes.

It's been a long winter . . . the winter is longing. Snow. snow. snowing. sun. sun. sunny. sleet. sun. slushy snow. Fragrant wetness clings to my thoughts and seeps down into the cavities of my molars until I eventually wince from winter's thaw flooding me.

The clouds stir mathematical sets, like a ladle to a pot of Jemez Pueblo red chile stew. The fragrant steam adheres to the bottom of my shoes. I hear it leave, using the entryway to my house. mirage. rainbow. white dawn.

milepost 54
hwy 491
dirt road 192
1¼ miles west

there you should find a house
with a red metal roof
the house
that contains
my Navajo Education

lesson 38
not a bar
not a casino
not a *hooghan*
it all began in a car
the kids are restless
tired of being confined to this holding tank
and this time it is cold
the dark cloudy mountains calculate early snow from
the restless kids
tired of telling jokes
tired of playing "I Spy"
tired of tribal radio

assignment 38
    1. diagram the separation
    2. write a poem about the language not spoken
    3. rearrange lines in symbolic order

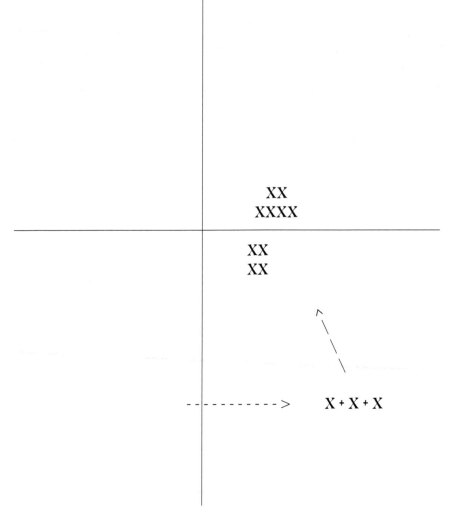

assignment 39

    1. analyze the separation

    2. write a poem about the language not spoken

    3. rearrange the diagram in symbolic order

formations, formulae

form
-ed
-ing

like bring – forth
the last born's – birthing
wind, winding up
an earthy landing in the next _____

After the Season of Big Wind: An Assay

The scene is not dreamlike. I don't see a sunrise. We are on the ocean's curved bottom wondering where all the water went. We are standing among the snarling sandstone monsters. We glance to the eastern horizon, searching. Where are the monster slayers?

Are freedom fighters on their way? My materialistic soft goods are hardened. Am I living the "American" dream?

I go to the south to immerse myself in the blue dust teachings. I connect the points of penetration like a child drawing in a learning tablet. The west side of my tablet is filled with songs and sand from the abundant Pacific Ocean. The gait in my footstep is rough like the churning water, life.

I am back in the north, my children's cords tether me near Dibé Ntsaa. We tether together. One mass of blood and tissue stemming from this place. The one I am standing on now. The one that pulses through the asphalt laded paths.

This mountain has folded my fight into a wind. My breath. My vocabulary. My wind whistling into the sharp edges of arrowheads.

The spring weather is dressed in the glistening language from abalone shells, the early seedlings murmur.

That is my introduction. I have just entered this world.

EAST

eastern

easterly, as ginger

Poplar, as wood

Juniper seeds, re-planted

bonfires, best —

with ocean waves, nearby

(hint: a place I call home)

Before We Ever Begin

         the code was prepared
         the formula measured
         droplet by droplet
each moist and breathing nucleus
expectant
expletive
explosive   —A glittering
world to draw upon

         The real beginning is
summer 1968
cesarean birth
urban Indian implanted
#311,990
injected with a propelling wind
a coiling vein
a pouch to carry pollen
those crossblood prayers
whispering from the kitchen
my husband calls home

          He shucks dried corn
          with a dull blade
          the tin can rings when
          kernels hit bottom

I sit in view
nibbling away
scrambled like
the eggs
in my tortilla

I sing prayer in silence
measuring my slow chewing
becoming each word
gnashing to death each swallow
believing he does the same

I watch him crank circles with the cast iron grinder
I watch him move into the spiraling ribbons of silence
I watch him funnel coarsely ground thoughts
        neatly packed and twist-tied in the transparent Ziploc bag

Our ceremony
opens with an aubade, *abiní bitsodizin*
white light showers us
stark into the valleys of years
we burdened
and caused burden
and fled

The bag of cornmeal
sits with us and waits
as we journey

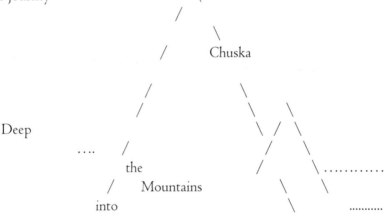

Deep

.... the Mountains into Chuska

among the pines (their concealed roots forming our spine)
        and the aspens (their conscious stare grasping my seedlings)
to retrace
the footprints of our past
the soles of our feet
walking toward the dark north
forward into unknown
extracting our past from this recipe
adding new ingredients to bless our future

Morning Song

Only the cat and I are awake
The birds become barely audible with dawn rising
Its white light cleanses our home, tumbling into our thoughts
Like machines that dictate arrivals and departures
I sit here and type – and wonder about Emily Dickinson
About the ink in her wells and the stains on her fingers

The morning song harmonizes as the sun is warming
The appliance hums – heavy, a slothful resonance
Percolating images, wonderfully hopeful petitions
Of daily prayer, piled high like chopped wood, rewarding
And oozing with fresh sap, spiraling from my fingertip pads –
Sometimes, tacky and sharply scented

New Dawning

Day I — StarMist Woman
I mourn for a woman trained under the United States of America Bureau of Indian Affairs, frayed ends of termination tightly woven into her story of relocation, into her bathing (and baking) techniques. As a child, she would rigidly scrub my small body with white bars of soap — meticulous, in her action, my body would sting and shine. Her memory and her trainings from boarding school, a patina on my limbs. The BIA gospel of Relocation: scraping the roots and transplanting them — the desired outcome a severing — scrambling the kernel within, each action choking the spirit, scrubbing the flesh, or the floors, the dishes, the laundry, the inside creases of landscape, folded and folded, into tiny pockets. Scrubbing each syllable off the tongue. Scrubbing as technique, until natural as a twitch. The relocated doctrine poses as a boxed gift, a wrapped layer of flesh and memory, a congressional sash as adornment.

She was my mother's older sister caught in the cold war construction of American —
a hybrid ceremony

          re-

                    located

— the acid in foreign soil

Do you remember that bunny cake she made for Easter?
sprinkled with shredded coconut
a rainbow of jellybeans bordered
the spongy masterpiece

Day 2 – Sassy Wood Mama
I am unfolding the intricacies of my own vessel
digging deep into lessons 1–24

I am in the midst of my own physical grime
I am drawing upon the groundwater of my allotment
I am tying my bundles
I am tying my bundles

Day 3 – StarMist Woman

the actors:

1. beauty
2. freedom
3. ceremony
4. sacrifice
5. youth
6. romance

the stage:

a place   some call California
a place   of mirage and machines

props:

discarded remnants
prized fibers of chance
bark from the Yosemite forest
abalone shell slivers
heathery saltbrush twine
cement and tar, and heavy metals

in the blackbox:

re-create home

Day 4 – Sassy Wood Mama
I am in that place of home: roasted beef baked potatoes afghan quilts
handwritten cards pocket money her place of home *I am with her*
attempting to replicate the recipes from her cookbook

I add the dark mist of coal-fire
white cream from milk and honey
childhood giants who occupy my land
punk rappers and checkerboarded fragments
the bitter roots coursing through my blood

I am building a new recipe
with adobe bricks
discarded rubber tires
rez-soaked tissue and membrane
reckless deviations from the enemy world

Last Day — SassyWood Mama mourns for StarMist Woman
starting with my belly (tastes and tolerances) convenience of genetically
modified products ingested as nutrition, by-products, unconscionable
movements, perhaps loss of sphincter control perhaps laboratory-contrived
responses, a preprogrammed conception, held in-trust by the USDA or the
BIA, Mission Control — electronically altering our environment motions and
decisions

StarMist Woman smiles
Just take a drive on the rez — sunny spring day with the latest Hopi reggae

Sassy —
Wood Mama would
search the night for new dawn
eager for the white light blessing
again

Still Life #1

Burnished morning light
A newlywed apartment
Japanese ceramic bowls nestled on open shelves
argent flatware tucked in bamboo drawers
products of folding a thousand paper cranes
a 1990s bouquet, the palest of pinks dried roses
splatterings of Silicon Valley binary code wallpaper
emitting a supplemental mineral
soluble in blood and adherent
to white lightning power surges

From the stiff midcentury chair, I sit on
the glowy light refracts the steam of
the peasant green tea I sip

swallowing the struggle of early spring
$\qquad\qquad\qquad\qquad\qquad$ becoming

(the in between)

you are in cosmic darkness
awaiting the morning light
you breathe and think, breathe
and watch your breath
zigzag into vibrations
nitsáhákees
pause (your breathing is thinking and your thinking is the shadowed mists)

      the medicine man laughs
      at his own jokes — *baa dloh hasin . . .*
      uses English to say
      I am doing fine
      I am doing fine!
      I am doing
      I am

jotting down the notes
columns

author	persona
author	persona
author	persona
bił bééhózín	~~persona~~
~~author~~	*dishni*
dooleeł	~~persona~~

The Rings Around Her Planet

I dreamed of Sappho of Lesvos and she was driving a Hummer, I cannot remember the color but it was parked very close to my minivan. I saw her talking with men from the naval base in Alameda, California. I asked her if she could move her Hummer and instead she gave me the keys. I drove around the lot until I found the perfect spot next to a brightly painted school bus with the question *"Is your world represented to the media?"* painted across it in bold red paint. Handing her back the keys, I noticed her skin was a gentle, glowing bronze, not at all the milky white color depicted in her portraits. Her hair was dark and bundled behind her skull, the perfect oval or the capital letter "O," symmetrical and fluid like her conversation. She wore jewelry made of shells and fastened with leather, reminiscent of the Yurok tribe in northern California who wear dentalium shells with abalone and intricate basket weavings. She was smoking a cigar while talking about the war and hand-to-hand combat. I know the men had no idea who she was. I wanted to show her a book of her published writing so she could fill in the blanks. She said she had no time, that she was running out of _____, that a _____ person was meeting her at the _____ at 4:15 pm.

(White) Interview

The linguist sits down
(click)
the sound recorder is breathing (rruuuh + rolllling)
humming the tune along the nearby canyon ridges

we listen
the silence breathes and empties
hollowing the elements
the first question rumbles (rruuuh + rolllling)
a song forms
nestles in the small swells, then
released from early spring sagebrush, the glossy tuft
chanting in rhythm to the raindrops (rruuuh + rolllling)
that flood, suspend, deepen, caress

the song floats above the Creator's hand
humming over the recorder's breath, the strife in newborn motion
filling, completing (rruuuh + rolllling)
don't ask me to sing it
don't ask me to disturb it
don't ask me
I don't know how to give a deserving grace, a triumphant
force to each white dawn morning
over and over, a renewal every day

SOUTH

Red-

wood

soil is

fertile

grow-

ing

roots

slowly

adding to

the southernly

transplants of LA

5−1=4//////////////

6−2=4////////////////

1+1+2//////////////////////

...........2+2................

............................4−0=4......+2..................

4

4

4

4

What do we bring back to the rez?
What is our offering?
A woman's moon full, brimming with blood
a newborn child's crimson
placental shell
scarlet red lips shaping
the iPod's mouth and
volume, speed
direction
the letter "i" chirping
and expanding its long
legs like wings
the pools of water
embedded into sandstone
                              are slowly satisfying
the ocean's thirst
for fresh water   squeezed

the wrenching lens renders two-dimensional
perversions, IHS prescriptions
that thin the blue lining
of my heart
the rising steam of
early morning roadkill

family pets
community pests, like
stencil-painted signs
of last week's
ACESWILD dance, like
a white-socked horse
crossing for the next
15 miles, like a
sheepherder stepping off
a faded school bus at
4:15 pm, the sheep and
shaggy goats settled by
the cattle guard, like a
grove of Russian olive
stumps

Still Life #2

A blazing midday sun
Walatowa summer heat
a line of Feast Day dancers

adobe-walled abodes
radiance aglow

Walatowa summer heat
red chile broth and crisp crust
slices of apple pie

The Albatross

Every day he walked into the Albatross, sliding into a corner booth. He usually waited several minutes before ordering his first drink. The several minutes of decision making always involved the first:

- a.   time he was struck by lightning
- b.   bite of a North Beach Pizza
- c.   droplets of sweat mixing into a dance club's pheromones
- d.   crisp October walk along the mesa's rim

Some days the minutes turned into stories he used as reference points to bring him back to his quiet corner booth. His aunt Lita told him once that he was abandoned because he was struck by lightning as an infant. That was the only time his heart skipped a beat, it felt like a kite. A strong desire to fly, not away or like a whirlwind. His desire was to spread across the planet with a force tumbling steady as a river.

Some days he would replay the dialogue that never made it past his heart. Like the time he just ate slice after slice of garlic pizza in a North Beach pizzeria when he should have been using his mouth to ask Lindsay to be his wife: *Remember the day we met? I was still so . . . and everything . . . new and different. I never had a . . . until you . . . and I wanted . . . never knew . . . you . . . rest of my life. I met you . . . I didn't think you . . . I didn't think it . . . I wonder why you . . . I hadn't thought . . . much before I moved here, and you. . . .* The gold wedding band nestled in his pocket all night and on into laundry day and on into the next laundry day until it was finally lost like all the one-sided socks that hung on the laundromat wall. Each month, the attendant displayed those lost socks into art – pinned and hung on the southernmost wall. He especially enjoyed the jack o' lantern in October.

Some days he just sat quietly, soaking in the sweet moisture from DJ Kirk threading the loop of everyone on the dance floor. It reminded him of the way his aunt patched his knee torn jeans. Her crisscross stitches were always done with her gigantic spool of rainbow thread. The needle became a lightning bolt weaving the rainbow's powers into his clothing. On the dance floor, the honey-scented steam fastened him to the circle – venomous nectar entered his pores and incensed his morning coffee.

Some days the October chill frosted his words like an empty vending machine. Sometimes he would wait in the cold until he was restocked. He wasn't really sure where his words went, compacted into combustible carbonated units or did his words spiral into thin coils of disks, bound neatly like masking tape? The sun's rays said, "My vibrations connect to your DNA." The Siberian elders chant in their cardboard twangy, high-pitched whistle, singing in their special way, communicating with the spirits standing outside. The 61,000 indigenous Horse People in Siberia are waiting for our answer; they are carrying an ornamental breastplate covering their exposed heart. The yellow stars gather at the peak of a sacred mountain. The scientists are speaking in theoretical explanations. "Your sickness is behind the wall." The ignored history is detailed in the Milky Way's placement. His whimpered question: "Learn the night chants. The Enemyway is just a song?" Colonization is just another mathematical theory trapped in the late harvesting of dried corn. And that dried corn simmers and stirs in a pot of winter stew months later, years later, or just minutes away.

Study on the Road to Los Angeles

Pass the power plant that
lights up Southern California
in sight of the Hogback ridge and
tucked in the New Mexico side
of the Four Corners
in the "American" southwest
where talk of the hot and dry desert is
always of conversation
just as common as morning greetings:
     Yá'át'ééh abíní, good morning
               Aoo', yá'át'ééh, yes, it is good

Pass the Chaco River that runs
with mountain snow from
the north
Headed west
traveling south first
on the infamous highway triple 6
greeted by the great mesa — a table for giants
     and the
friendly spiny-ridged dinosaurs
placed just so . . .

(It is this area
that the family of an adulteress lives)

. . . then *shiálchíní binalí bighan*
Newcomb, New Mexico

Dootł'izh is all around us:
the summer sagebrush
rectangular mile markers
hazy sky
the dark silhouette of the cool Chuska Mountains
the old rez truck with the missing tailgate

even the bald spare tire on the truck is blue
lots of rez rides
not so many RVs or semis
then a prairie dog scampers across
                              the hot pavement
At Sheepsprings
the car windows all rolled down
the HUD housing marks the turnoff to the paved road
that divides the Chuskas
A/C couldn't make this day any cooler

The sun
right above the cracked windshield
provides
perfect light and shadow
to writing utensil
she'awéé' sleeps
in a modern cradleboard that meets
car and airplane safety requirements

So far only one hitchhiker
an elder woman too tired
to hold out her thumb, only one
tribal police car
At the Crownpoint turnoff
      Torreon lies farther east fringing the checkered
eastern outskirts of the rez
One UPS truck and
the highway expands to
a double-laner, almost to Gallup

Then
west on Interstate 40
Flagstaff only 185 miles ahead
the cool evening glow from
the Grand Canyon State mellows
the first book on tape, *Crow Dog*:
"We've got to civilize the white man
because they have gone crazy!"

Memories of *shizhé'é*
Rugged as the Arizona desert
untamed and rough

                          unbearable yet free

with
piercing
and steamy
hot days
all forgotten when the sun sets
when the coolness cools
thoughts into a latitudinal glow

hózhó
peace, beauty
complete
San Francisco Peaks in the distance
tummy no longer rumbling
heart pumping
children needing to pee and stretch

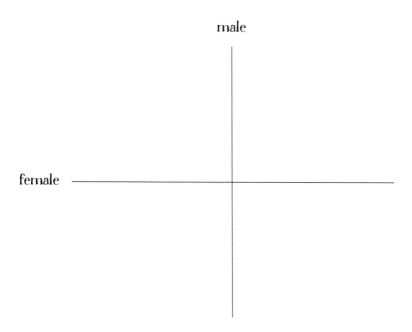

male

female

salt water   1956   Two-Way Inn
1978   bicycle   East LA
popcorn   East Bay   Johnny Shrimp
4 corners   199_   stick-shift truck

assignment 43
1. find the complementary points
2. plot the coordinates at their intersection
3. use the visual text created as a key for diagrams

(Blue) Interview

the questions – a diaspora like late summer tumbleweeds
    a whisper: if their breath is the moisture that sharpens the barbs
        silence: if unformed and pliable – beneath thoughts

a discourse: if in constant suspension, a nest of kept coordinates, logged as
locations, numbers – steadfast to the original pattern

O to be the one with the master key

Dootłizh

Christmas day
we sat at the ocean along the Southern California coast
the loud voices in the waves
made our own anger seem ridiculous, a tantrum

our tears like breakers of unsaid sayings
an orbital crash pounding
surface into sandstone
a mortar and pestle, rhythmic as each change in tide

How fascinating the light glows
crystal in places
deep with envy in others
and still dark with mystery, like the language

within
releasing true colors
or maybe not
dootł'izh

Navajo language
where blue is green and green is blue
churning a color into living water, an ocean
or perhaps union . . .

Dootł'izh
like the churning waters
Dootł'izh
like the churning waters

The Bundling . . .

I am settling into the season of rest
no more hauling wood
it is hard to be inside a dwelling for such long periods of time

it is easy to be inside a dwelling for such long periods of time
no more hauling water
I am settling into the season

Into the West

My little sister's boyfriend is a real Hollywood Indian. He even plays one in the Steven Spielberg miniseries, "Into the West: Journey to the Heart of the American Dream." So I said, "Does that mean you're now an Indian Princess by association?" She doesn't laugh but hands me a DVD set of the miniseries. We sit under a gazebo at the Sushi House in west Los Angeles. I swallow the last mouthful of genmai cha and take the gift. The bitter tailings of the tea intrigue me to ask what kind of role her boyfriend, Victor, plays. I can easily see Victor bare chested sitting upon a stallion screaming out a war cry. His long thick hair neatly woven into braids rests on his honey-colored chest. A stripe of red *chíih* across each cheekbone, maybe some on his horse. What Hollywood does not tell is that this war cry is not a declaration to war but a recurring nightmarish cry of waking up to the silence that sits heavy upon the heart like a ghost. Walking a mountain footpath full of pine cones and having each one a bloodline that no longer runs through veins. "Victor plays a very important role, he has a speaking part." I say, "Wow, they actually let him talk while he's scalping a helpless homesteader." I see her slow grin surface and she says, "Just watch it, he has a much bigger role than the one he had in *Smoke Signals*." Later, I watch Disc One with my husband. We eat popcorn and wince at the narrator, whose skin is pale like goose flesh, telling a Photoshop version of how our land was stolen. The narrator is Hollywood also, trying to be objective about the style in which Congress passed the Indian Removal Act of 1830, the Trail of Tears in 1838, the Fort Laramie Treaty of 1851. The narrator reveals thin attempts to resolve his conscience later in the episode for assisting a runaway slave and marrying a widowed Lakota woman he rescued from the auction block. I start to fold into the crisp scenery and romantic view of our idealistic beginning. Most people can't, but I can always spot the warrior, the chief or holy man crawling from the depths of Indian Alley, crawling from the animated screen back into a makeshift dwelling on downtown streets, cultural preservationists keeping vigilant watch over their bundles. As the sun sets on the first layer in this journey, the narrator's creamy voiceover blows the visionary history of Hollywood into my hair: "We have a wheel that goes from here to there. They have a wheel that goes to the stars."

my dreams tilt toward the

west, yet my prayers are drilled deep,

tethered to my home

WEST

Westernized

west+ward=me

west coast

water(full)

I keep my language in my back pocket like a special handkerchief that I only display when I want to show my manners in a respectful way

It is always so nice
to hear my language, even if
I don't fully understand it

I know when
someone is telling
someone else off

I know when
someone is telling
a joke, especially if it's about me

I know when
someone is being gentle, or kind
or gossiping and planting barbed seeds
with hushed voices

I know when
I am being reprimanded
"Yádiláh!"
"Doo ja'níí da!"

I know when
people are talking about my children
Don doo Esther biyazhi, bee álchíní
Desbah, Sǫ' Abini, Shandíín doo awéé'yazhi Marie

It is our great
Navajo language, Diné bizaad
that keeps me silent with hózhó, peace, beauty
even if

I am walking in downtown Los Angeles
among the Nakaii dine'é, Bináá'ádaalts'ózí
or Naakai Łizhinii

Their words and language
pass overhead
joining the thin outline of smog

I walk on
mumbling some Spanish, Japanese, Lakota or Crow
leaving them in thought about my origin

In the middle of busy intersections
and energy-efficient street lights
they see a cornfield and canyon walls

Bedazzled

I can give LA a vision
but does it want one?

another
highlight
in its overprocessed
dermis

a reason to pull off the road
graffiti the billboards with caller ID
petition gray matter with embryonic
patterns of absorption

I am not afraid to give LA
my vision
or my telephone number
census number
number of births
                            and deaths
recurrent
blood and tissue
spilt and tainted
twilight sun anointed
and aligned
squeezing my vision
into last season's shoes

My frame follows
cracks in the windshield
the electrical storm above the Jemez Mountains

My frame
billows and contours
shaping my spine
a sunbeam attached to the earth

volcanic
feverish
                    and bubbling
bubbling
and passing
over

The Birthed and the Birthing Years

I.

Our drive back home exposes bindings — a single-threaded needle binds me from the Groovyland of Southern California back home to my life at the base of the La Plata Mountains

Adaptation or migration — a toxicology screen for relocation (amp)utation — a governmental tangram

 — urban Indians — their pulsing lattice of new blood, a binding vine with delicate flowers emerging from cement cracks

A flavor, a memory: a bowl of mutton and dumplings, a hint of bitterroot, ground beef and potatoes with gravy, fire-charred tortillas, the spitfire engine of a pickup, hauling water, wood or children, counting stars from the back of that same pickup, the first time driving that pickup, 13 years old fighting with the squeaky clutch

2.

Evolution is wrong — we were always here the same as when we were first created with all imperfections in place perhaps we have even perfected those shortcomings into a shell as the tortoise our flesh our weakness our shell the world growing thicker with each battle every boundary crossed or delineated etched into our backs our history carved into this shell interpretation unnecessary translation impossible a display of beauty and long suffering tedious with technique depositing layers toxic waste perhaps seeping deeper and deeper closer to flesh the waste a monolith a pattern of insomnia the relocated flesh its own compass following the map on its back

3.

The penetrating summer heat wrestles the autumnal clouds rushing forward like tongues spreading rumors as my two eldest daughters play in the muddy clay banks of the San Juan River

Soon the sticky riverbank will harden and the cradling lull will lapse, longing for mountain snow water, for conversation like Cameron chapter meetings

My offspring laugh and whisper, the canyon echoes bounce back and forth and back and forth until the words fade, layers of contour to the high sandstone walls, a contribution to beauty and history

4.
The woman (with the long, tight, permed hair) and the cowboy (who towered at least a foot above her)

Filled with sorrow, his moustache drooped with his frown as he picked up his black felt hat off the floor

She knocked that black hat off his head, saying, "That's the way *you* wanted it!" – but the real assault came from her attitude and anger, her words didn't seem to mean much

She left (walked out of the McDonald's restaurant in K-town), her curly hair bouncing behind her

I saw her climb into a shiny Ford F250 four-wheel-drive pickup and drive off leaving the cowboy (her cowboy) standing bewildered, he pretended to read the newspaper clenched in his fists (when people stared) and straightened his hat glancing out the window, then skimmed through the rodeo section of the paper wondering if his next opportunity at love was just a bull ride away

About ten minutes later people quit staring finding greater interest in their value-sized meals while the cowboy, tired of pacing the floor, threw his paper on one of the tables and headed for the door just as that shiny Ford pickup pulled up, and that cowboy straightened his hat walked out to the truck and climbed in

(Yellow) Interview

laughter spirals out before I even ask the questions . . .

. . .

. . .

. . .

. . .

like twins who wrestle in the womb

. . .
like squash blossoming

An Example of Bundling from
Earth-Surface Dwellers

I said yes there was a time I thought
we were lovers, walking each footstep
like a mold, a semblance we were able to
live by, a next door neighbor who knew

we occasionally swore and smoked pot and
waltzed naked in our clothes, a cashier
from the market scanning pints of mint
chip ice cream, bottles of locally brewed

beer, assorted glass jars, muted hues
of uncooked grains — or the Rasta vendor
at the flea market who overheard me
saying, "I love you" when I didn't, I didn't

want it to be like a bed, like tucked into a bed —
into the years I can't recall, the lining of my
panty drawer, how the reflected sun colored our
hair, a temporary dye from when we were lovers

Soft Goods Bundles

I.

My husband and I are waking up early so we can practice couple's yoga. We tangle our limbs and laugh, shake the leaves that expose our twisted trunks. When he cannot sleep, he reads poetry to me. His deep voice covers the top half of my sky—softness like pastel sheets and a comfortable pillow, a thunderbolt cracks as he pauses between syllables.

2.
The female rain calms
the oozing heat in my mid—
section dampened pine
perfumed sap clinging to four
hours of moonbeam ripening

3.
Indian summer days—
fat, ripe, sun-kissed haze

corn pollen smudged rays
goldenrod sachet

Indian summer days—
some calm, some ablaze

balmy sandstone plays
tricks, to hold my gaze

Autumn Time

The glittering part of the day deepens. Speckled sheets of gray.
Periwinkle washes. The steady whip of wind, gaining, climaxing.

> *"You were talking in your sleep. You were calling someone's*
> *name, Seymore, Stephen, started with an 'S.'"*
> *I didn't think I talked in my sleep. I barely remember dreams. I*
> *said, "Stacey." I was talking to my former student on the phone*
> *last night.*
> *He said, "No, it was a man."*
> *I said nothing. I thought everything. I mumbled, twisting with the*
> *sheets of gray overhead.*

The nights toss around in the field between our
tangled legs. 20 years of it. A house. children. dog. cats. turtle.
My job(s). His work. My slips of paper – tornado scrawled fragments
– jagged like
the way he chips at stone

releasing flood waters like an irrigated field between our legs
a bed of summer flowers blooming
bellowing, squashed
a deluged fragrance

like a microburst held captive.

> The St. Joseph's Indian School is writing me again. What do
> I tell them? I have four hungry Indian children of my own to
> feed, clothe, and protect:
> *God in heaven, protect the children*
> *that I can't. Wrap the sparkle of the*
> *Milky Way into their clothing, into*
> *their thoughts . . . Dear Children of St.*
> *Joseph's, I pray that God will spread*
> *the last bits of harvest, that the*
> *fragrance of a bountiful garden will*
> *nourish you like a star quilt during*
> *winter months.*
> *And thank you for the personalized*
> *address labels and shiny stickers.*

Kǫ'

I wonder at the color of the heart, the way it whispers
and bears all things, digs deeper
to will the mountain within the stone, such pleasure
created between two
natural as the moment of conception
wrinkled into the pocket of a jacket no longer worn, yet

stores the tender moments of light
each day
I complicate my development
calling on a social order as appropriate
My real map marks the births of my four children
Along my spine, I still feel their tingle

My womb aches, a hollow tree
yearning for the birds that no longer nest there
A whirlwind trails circles around my middle
and sometimes is my only memory, *kǫ'*
the spirit of fire, walks

and now whispers into its own hearth
My heart glows to see that *kǫ'* in my children
that blaze of blood mixing, *hózhónííyee'*
soft moist breath, *kǫ'*
like spirals and whirls, just stirring it up

NORTH

anchored and folded

the rainbow's rays prepare me

grown, grounded and firm

(Black) Interview (with the Anthropologist)

my stronghold lies in the (un)articulated folds
of my dark, lengthy hair
I hold the thinkingness captive
feasting on the (un)assembled, cozy as charcoal fire
The gathering of springtime-scented theory
into small packets, like seeds
maybe for a winter garden
maybe for trade
maybe

the anthro is germinating, loosening
clothing, scratching irritations and
then finally
dipping his bread into the bone broth

During My Evening Chores

In soft spaces between the light and shadow, I soaked
into the page of the sky, sumi ink on rice paper
bleeding, spread thin across the horizontal span

I found myself smeared and thin as the clouds
not sure of my calling – perhaps a charge
to collect, collate the circular dialogue, catalogue

the coarseness in strands of hair, spiraling from
taut corners of shortened daylight, the folds
of early night fall, and the gentlest northeast wind

sidling across my tail bone. Under cloud
cover, I rest and waddle about my sloshy inkwell
thin and thick as twilight

Night Song

Here under the dark moon a melody distills through my breath. All night its vapors gleaned in my larynx and sang. Certain few whispered a low chorus and felt as if they were being serenaded by their first love, a song new mothers hang in the nursery beside the child's christening layette gown. *Please, remember to bring the song home!* The melody circles through the dampness of summer monsoons and lands like a piece of autumn fruit to a tree. Sweet juices gulped down into a hungry throat, the whisper forgotten as the pulling tide of winter sleep nestles beneath the belly, inside the spongy marrow along the spine. Yet those with insomnia gather all their threads of consciousness tangled to medicine cabinets, *What does two tablets twice daily really mean?* In the ink-stained moon, the whisper is the trickle in the nearby mountain stream, churning lightly, becoming the breezy drafts at windowsills. Listen: it is the dull ache in the black bars across the top half of a mackerel's body, its oily flesh clogging coastal rivers. Listen: it is the Jemez Pueblo red chile powder waxing the moon, the seismic undercurrent of the black eagle's wings. Listen.

Atmospheric Correction

After a photo of 19 Hopi men imprisoned at Alcatraz Island for refusing to send their children to federally run boarding schools and to farm using techniques prescribed by federal officials. Originally thought to be Apache, the men are referred to as "Moqui Indians" in the photograph.

Transparent and syrupy days. Fading LA smog.
The bed of dentalium. Heat from San Jacinto's hips.
The photo entitled, "Moqui Indians, 1895." The overlay

"Urban Indians, 2016" burned-in. Entitlement stamped
in gelatin. "Prisoners they shall stay until they have
learned to appreciate the advantages of education."

Alcatraz Island. ". . . until they shall evince, in an
unmistakable manner, a desire to cease interference
with the plans of the government for the civilization

and education of the Indian wards." Masatiwa,
Sikyakeptiwa, Lomayestiwa. 19 Indians with ink-
stained fingers. Their prints pressed into the

rock walls. Their heritage into my blueprints,
stamped Bureau of Indian Affairs. Called Department of
War. Sherman Institute. Riverside, California.

Heat from San Jacinto's hips settled in thermal mineral
pools of ink-stained fingers. Burned in LA smog. Dodged
out Urban Indian. Fading Indian, fading.

The Menu:

nímasii, ayeezhii, na'jahá	*potatoes, eggs, spam*
náneeskaadí	*tortilla*
gohwééh	*coffee*
dibé bitoo'	*mutton stew*
che' diyaan	*frybread*
tódilchxoshí	*pop*
atsi' sit'ée	*roast turkey*
ditldí	*Jell-O*
báá likaní yazhi	*cookies*
alkaan	*Navajo Cake*

The author record (-ed, -ing) as Navajo Tradition. Repeat as needed.

Gone

I.
to the reservation
today, left a basket
full, carrying a basket
carrying the ochre sand residue
thin barbs of wind
burnt umber willow marring the bow
in my back

                                        Gone
                            like the reservation today,
                                        gone
                                        as in
                            the "gooder days shoulda been
                                        better"
                                        than
                            ambidextrous texts
                                    elapsing
                                        our
                                        time
                            linear bullet points
                                    and bold
                                        print
                            rising like early morning
                                    phlegm
                                    tinged
                                burnt umber
                                then gone —
                        Our basket empty again

2.
We've been traveling so long on this highway
We forget our image in the Route 66 rock and mineral store
We forget our language in the static of radio waves
We forget why we travel, the feast days are tourist pit stops
Carnival vendors woven into the millennium manta

This highway—so long, has been traveled
The rock and minerals become our image
The static in our language transcends over radio
The usual pit stops are touristy, flooded like arroyos during
Monsoon season, the Shiprock Fair during election year

3.

In one breath I try to say all that has been said in the last 500 years, I don't want to go back any further, I don't want to think back any more, I want to spread my four treasures across the page like a belly dancer, moving between light and shadow, exposing all the necessary parts

4.

There was never a sound beside the smoke but from it
A weeping being whispered into the ground
What was it it whispered?
I could tell you it was chants we use in ceremonies
I could tell you it was the truths my father cursed when he was drunk
I could tell you there is no translation

no words exist for that whisper

Perhaps all these thoughts are correct, crystal as the cracks in the windshield,
tearful as the mom of four who sits in her
car, pondering over the latest IHS doled prescription drug
Or something about
Possibilities in situations exponentially simmering
Branching into multiple choice responses/answers
Or silences/voids
The weeping hangs like the hind legs of a slaughtered goat,
And whispers droplets of blood
Thick
Draining from the headless animal
Splattered on the ground

The Diameter of the Bomb

After a poem from Yehuda Amichai with the same title.

For Joe Edd and his family

The initial blast at least two generations deep
shrapnel rupturing the patriarch bloodline,
leaving one dead and fourteen wounded
one still in the womb

Cedar smoke to offset the implosion, yet no
effective remedy for the shock
wave – fragmented pain, fierce
and smothering as a riptide

The grieving crossed arroyo flood waters to
bury a combat soldier, west of Canyon Diablo
under the shade of the Abalone Shell Mountain
over three hundred miles away

Secondary debris fractures the breastbone,
arrests the heart of a lone child, weeping
in a far corner of a middle-school dance, gently
tying bundles, pleas, petitions, a pronouncing

Of all the cries, shaky and ceremonious, a wailing,
a laceration of soft tissue sheltered by the rainbow's arc
folding darkness into darkness into the glittering cosmos
into the restorative white dawn

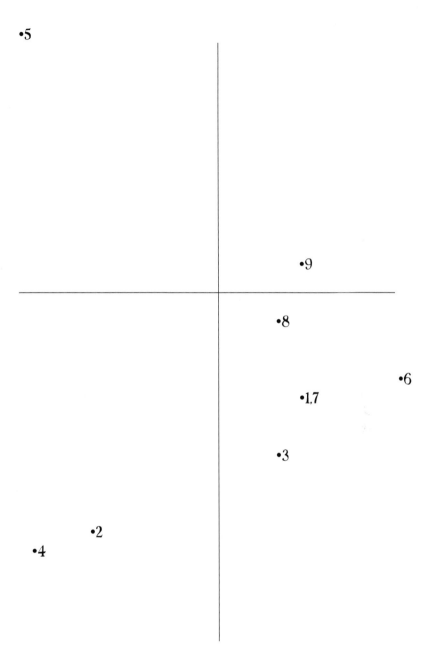

Relocate as needed

Bind   Tie   Bind   Tie   Bind   Tie   Small   Bind-ed
     -ing   Wood   Water
       Binding   Fire(in)Sky
~~Binding~~   the   Sky——— ~~Binding~~   Skies
~~Binding~~ the   Skies(Waters)
     Bound   and   unraveled   and   bound
And   (of)Wood   and Skies and bound and
     Unravelling   the   Sky
———— ~~Unravelling~~   Sky
———— ~~Unravelling~~   ~~the~~(in)   (Waters)~~Skies~~
Unravelling   our(Fire)   and   Skies
     and Bind   (-ed, -ing)   Tie   Bind   Tie   Bound

Assignment 44

Analyze the above conversation. Read it aloud. Read it loudly. Weave a thread through it. Bind your bundle of sayings, be mindful of loose strands. Smooth down frayed edges. Smudge with fire or water.

Extra Credit: Take the relocated points from the previous diagram and use them as an entryway.

PREVIOUSLY PUBLISHED POEMS

"Ko'": earlier version published in *The Iowa Review* (2001)

"Dootł'izh": earlier version published in *Frontiers: A Journal of Women Studies* (2002)

"4+4+4+4 divided": published under different title in *Wicazo Sa Review* (2007)

"An Example of Bundling from Earth-Surface Dwellers": published as "Ceremony #3" in *Red Ink* (Spring 2008)

"The Rings Around Her Planet": published in *Sentence* (2010)

"Gone": published in *Prairie Schooner* (Winter 2012)

Sections of "bundles are bundling": previously published as "Separation" in *Stray Dogs: Writing from the Other America* (2014)

ABOUT THE AUTHOR

ESTHER G. BELIN is an artist and poet. Her latest work is a personal study of abstract realism and a flesh-burdened reality. Belin graduated from the University of California at Berkeley, the Institute of American Indian Arts in Santa Fe, New Mexico, and Antioch University in Los Angeles. In 2000, she won the American Book Award for her first book of poetry, *From the Belly of My Beauty*. Belin is a citizen of the Diné nation, which is enveloped inside the southwestern United States. She lives on the Colorado side of the Four Corners.

www.estherbelin.com